Original title:
The Fruitful Path

Copyright © 2025 Creative Arts Management OÜ
All rights reserved.

Author: Simon Fairchild
ISBN HARDBACK: 978-1-80586-442-4
ISBN PAPERBACK: 978-1-80586-914-6

## Nature's Palette of Possibilities

In a garden bright with glee,
Tomatoes dance with jubilee.
Cucumbers wear a floppy hat,
While radishes do a silly chat.

Berries bounce on the green grass,
Wishing they could take a pass.
Peppers boast in colors bold,
Who knew veggies could be so old?

In the trees, bananas swing,
Telling tales of goofy things.
Apples giggle, pears take flight,
Saying, "Life is pure delight!"

As the sun sets, fruits unite,
With a party full of light.
Munching joy, they reach the stars,
Who knew snacks could have such czars?

**Seeds of Serendipity**

In a garden filled with laughter,
I planted seeds of joy.
They sprouted up in patterns loud,
And danced like a silly boy.

The tomato claimed to know a joke,
While carrots wore a grin.
The pumpkin's puns were quite a hit,
And made our hearts spin.

## Journey Through Orchards

Strolling through the apple grove,
I tripped on a pear.
Fell right into a pile of prunes,
And that was quite a scare!

The trees were gossiping up high,
About the funniest fruit.
A grape slipped up, fell on its vine,
And rolled off in pursuit.

**Unripe Visions**

Banana dreams of daring feats,
But still wears a green hue.
It tries to leap, the peel slips out,
And it whines, "Oh what to do?"

An avocado splits a pun or two,
Saying, "I'm the guac of town!"
But when asked for a dance-off,
It's too afraid to get down!

## Sweet Whispers of Growth

Berries whispered secrets sweet,
As blossoms spun around.
"Let's tell the world our silly tales,
In every shape and sound!"

Watermelons had a pep talk,
While laughter filled the air.
They juggled seeds and giggled loud,
Without a single care.

## **Threads of Greenery**

In a garden where socks grow on trees,
We dance with the ants and chat with the bees.
Mismatched shoes sprout, oh what a sight!
Who knew that weeds could be so polite?

A cucumber wearing a jaunty hat,
Said, 'Join me for tea; I've a fancy mat!'
Mirthful mushrooms play hopscotch at dawn,
As the giggles of carrots stretch far and beyond.

## Seasonal Adventures

In winter, we skate on the frozen pears,
Building snowmen with the fluffiest hairs.
Summer brings pies made of sun-kissed fruit,
While dances with cherries suit every boot.

O autumn, you trick us with pumpkins so bright,
We try to carve faces but start quite a fight.
Spring brings the flowers, all pink and quite silly,
But tulips tell jokes that are rather frilly.

## Glade of Aspirations

In a glade where dreams sprout like beans,
Frogs wear tuxedos, oh what funny scenes!
The daisies debate the best way to grow,
While a wise old toad sings of ebb and flow.

Bunny entrepreneurs sell carrots online,
While raccoons host parties with sparkling wine.
Each whisper of hope floats on the breeze,
As shadows stretch out and dance with great ease.

**Sweetness of Solitude**

In a quiet nook filled with chocolate delight,
Lollipops gossip while snuggled up tight.
Marshmallows bounce in a cozy embrace,
Oh, sweetness of solitude, what a fine place!

With gummy bears crafting a palace so grand,
The jellybeans giggle and lend a soft hand.
Here in this haven, the world seems so bright,
Where candy canes dream of taking flight.

## Lush Echoes of the Heart

In gardens wild, the gnomes do dance,
Hoping that tomatoes will have a chance.
With carrots dressed in coats of green,
They wait for light, but sleep, unseen.

A slug in shades, a snail in style,
Both take their time, but with a smile.
While bunnies hop and munch away,
They laugh at seeds that went astray.

## **Fields of Promise**

In fields of corn, the cobs do cheer,
With popcorn dreams that draw so near.
The scarecrow plays a flute at night,
While crows join in to share the fright.

Sunflowers tilt, just like a hat,
Chasing the sun, where's it at?
They whisper jokes in breezy tones,
While ants march on their tiny phones.

## Among the Ripening Leaves

Leaves rustle secrets of summer's tease,
As apples giggle, swaying in the breeze.
Beneath a branch, a pear sings low,
About a peach that stole the show.

A watermelon rolls with a belly laugh,
Joining the orchard in comedic half.
The figs play cards with a hapless prune,
While lemons zest just to lighten the tune.

**Nature's Silent Symphony**

In gardens grand, the tunes unfold,
With veggies jamming, bold and gold.
Beets drop bass, while peas do pop,
Flirting with radishes as they hop.

Orchards hum with laughter sweet,
As berries rehearse a berry beat.
Funny vines twist in a jig,
While nature smiles, it's quite a gig.

**The Sweetness of Every Step**

I tripped on a banana peel,
Yet laughter is what I feel.
Fruits rolling by, oh what a scene,
An orchard's dance, so fresh and green.

Maybe I'll run, but with a catch,
A watermelon's my clumsy match.
Each step I take, a juicy fate,
In this fruity world, I can't be late.

## **Echoes of Nurtured Souls**

There once was a pear who sang,
With every note, the garden swang.
Tomatoes chuckled, a fine old bunch,
As cucumbers practiced their brunch crunch.

A joke from the grapefruit caused a smile,
While carrots danced in gala style.
In this patch where veggies confide,
Each vegetable shares their joyful pride.

**Flourishing Amongst Thorns**

Roses giggled at their prickly fate,
While the daisies pondered, 'Are we late?'
Thorns were just the roses' jest,
In nature's play, they are the best.

Chickens clucked in a thicket's mess,
Finding seeds, oh what a quest!
Laughter blooms where thorns reside,
In every snag, there's joy inside.

## **Paving Roads with Petals**

A path of petals, soft and bright,
Led me to mushrooms dancing in light.
Snails made music, oh what a groove,
Each squishy step made my heart move.

With ladybugs on a sunny stroll,
And ants carrying snacks, they're on a roll.
In this jam session of garden prance,
Nature's humor leads the dance.

## Notes from the Orchard

There once was a pear with a knack,
It danced on the branch, that's a fact.
It twirled with a grin,
As apples joined in,
And all of the fruits kept on whack.

A banana slipped down in a rush,
Causing a nearby peach to hush.
They giggled and gawked,
While the cherries all talked,
And laughed 'til they turned into mush.

But then came a fruit fly with flair,
Who buzzed through the sweet-scented air.
She charmed all the crew,
With a jig that she knew,
Spreading laughter and sweet, juicy care.

So here in the grove, joy did sprout,
With antics that made folks shout.
For life in the trees,
Is a laugh and a breeze,
With every fruit's chuckle about.

## **Horizon of Harvest**

A zucchini dreamed of the stars,
Thinking maybe he'd travel to Mars.
But all of his friends,
Said, "Zuke, just make bends,
We prefer our own Earthly bars!"

Tomatoes were tasked with a show,
To prove they could dance to and fro.
They jiggled with flair,
In the sun's golden glare,
While cucumbers watched with a glow.

The corn popped up with a grin,
Saying, "Let the fun times begin!"
But then it got wild,
Like a mischievous child,
And chaos did swiftly set in.

So harvesters laughed in delight,
As veggies took flight in mid-night.
With jokes to display,
In a fresh, silly way,
The field became quite the sight.

**Pondering in the Canopy**


An apple pondered the weather,
Wondering if its leaves would tether.
"Should I wear a coat?"
It said with a note,
"Or just chill in this sunny together?"

The oranges smiled on the tree,
Sublime in their zesty esprit.
They said with a grin,
"Just let the sun in,
And laugh 'til you're rolling with glee!"

A grape hanging low in its clump,
Grew tired and wanted a jump.
So with a big leap,
It made all to weep,
As it landed, a total fruit thump.

So here in the canopy, cheer,
Each fruit pushed away all the fear.
With laughter in flow,
And silliness grow,
They danced through the bright atmosphere.

## **Echoes of Enchantment**

In the orchard where laughter would sing,
A mango wore crowns made of bling.
It strutted and spun,
Thinking, "Aren't I fun?"
While all of the berries did cling.

The almonds all gathered around,
To witness the moment profound.
"Let's start a new jam,"
Said the ever-sweet ham,
As we all made a wacky new sound.

Then the coconut joined in the spree,
With coconuts bobbing with glee.
They played hide and seek,
Where giggles would peek,
In a world full of fruit jubilee.

So echoes of joy filled the air,
As fruits joined together with flair.
With laughter bestowed,
Through the magical road,
They danced and they floated with care.

**Duet of the Seasons**

Spring sings loud, with flowers in tow,
While winter whispers, "Oh, no, no, no!"
Summer's a party, with ice cream galore,
And fall trips on leaves that dance on the floor.

The squirrel in spring is a real nutty chap,
In summer, he's busy napping on a map!
Autumn gives chests for all the nuts found,
While winter just grumbles, feeling quite drowned.

## Sowing Seeds of Tomorrow

Planters at dawn, in pajamas they creep,
Awkwardly tripping while trying to leap.
Seeds fly in circles, like birds in a fight,
"Just one right pluck!" they eagerly bite.

In the garden, a gnome with a mischievous grin,
Watches the chaos, just waiting to win.
The tulips argue, with petals held high,
While the onions just cry, "We've got to try!"

## Radiance Among the Shadows

A banana shines bright in the dimmest of nights,
While apples plot mischief with stealthy delights.
Grapes quietly giggle, all squushed in a bag,
Saying, "Why not squabble? It's fun when we tag!"

Under moonlit skies with a cheesy old grin,
Pumpkin decides it's time to begin.
He rolls to the party and slips on his skin,
"I'm the king of the fruit bowl, let the antics begin!"

## Marvels in the Mundane

A pickle once danced in a jar full of brine,
Hoping to be the next great headline.
Tomatoes roll in, with big juicy dreams,
"Let's start a band!"—oh, how silly it seems!

Lettuce in shades that are wildly sublime,
Claims it finds flavor, caught in a rhyme.
Through sprouting adventures, they laugh in the day,
Finding bliss in the mundane, come what may!

## Compass of Sweetness

In a world where candy grows,
And gummy bears wear tiny clothes,
I chased a peach that rolled away,
It laughed and danced, oh what a day!

Bananas whisper secrets sweet,
While apples tap their little feet,
With every bite, a giggle spills,
As cherries plot their sticky thrills.

A donut tree stood tall and round,
With sprinkles raining on the ground,
I climbed to taste the frosted sun,
And found a cupcake, oh what fun!

So follow fruits and don't delay,
The sweetness calls us, come and play,
With laughter as our compass guide,
We'll roam the orchard far and wide!

## **Canopy of Blessings**

Beneath the trees, a fruit parade,
With lemons pulling off charades,
While apricots swing from the vine,
The party starts, all is divine.

A watermelon wears dark shades,
While kumquats dance in upbeat spades,
The oranges juggle with delight,
As pineapples spin, what a sight!

"Grab a peach, let's have a feast!"
Yelled the grapes, "Join in, at least!"
They rolled around in juicy schemes,
While cherries plotted fruity dreams.

Under this vibrant, wacky roof,
We'll share a laugh, here's the proof:
Life's a blast with fruits like these,
So join our fun, if you please!

## Fragments of Fruition


In a bowl of melons and cheer,
A pineapple sang for all to hear,
It crooned a tune of sugary brio,
While coconut whispered soft and low.

The grapes had formed a marching band,
With rhythm and beats, the finest hand,
Each bite a thrill, a burst of joy,
In this fruity world, no time to be coy.

While tangy limes competed loud,
To prove their zest and make us proud,
The apples chuckled, rolling wide,
Inviting all to join the ride.

So gather 'round, let's eat and play,
With fragments of bliss, come what may,
In the orchard of fun, we unite,
Where fruity laughter takes its flight!

## Oasis of Possibilities

In a desert of snacks, we found our way,
To an oasis where bananas sway,
With dates that dance and figs that flip,
This is the land of fruity trip.

A cactus turned into a chocolate cake,
With sprouted berries, what a break!
The figs told jokes, they were so sly,
As we munched away, time flew by.

The peaches took a joyful leap,
While coconuts promised secrets to keep,
With every bite, a burst of glee,
An oasis where we all feel free.

So pack your bags, let's hit the trail,
In our land of fruit, we cannot fail,
With laughter, dreams, and fruity schemes,
We'll find our joy in the sweetest dreams!

## Between Petals and Promise

In gardens where the daisies dance,
The weeds have all taken a chance.
A snail with swagger, moving slow,
Claims the title of garden pro.

With squirrels plotting acorn schemes,
And butterflies on giddy dreams,
The tulips giggle in delight,
As bees take off in silly flight.

A worm in shades, quite dapper too,
Waves at flowers, a wacky crew.
They gossip 'neath the chatter tree,
Creating laughter naturally.

So wander through this sunny maze,
Where humor blooms in silly ways.
Between petals bright, a grand charade,
Life's fertile jokes, all hand-made.

## Unseen Riches

Beneath the soil, the treasures hide,
Where carrots boast of their sweet pride.
The radishes with rosy cheeks,
Hold gossip sessions for a week.

The moles with maps of secret spots,
Trade rumors with the tie-dye pots.
A cabbage claims to be a king,
While gallivanting in leafy bling.

The potatoes in their earthy lair,
Organize a dance without a care.
With each cartwheel, they seem to say,
"We're the stars of tuber ballet!"

So dig a little, laugh a lot,
Unseen prizes in the plot.
With roots that giggle, laugh away,
Finding joy in the soil's play.

## Riddles of the Garden

A cucumber asked a tomato,
"Why do you blush, oh, dear amigo?"
"It's not just me, the radishes too,
We're all in style—are you, boo?"

The carrots whisper, 'Is it a plot?'
While peas in pods are quite distraught.
"We can't keep up with all this style,"
Murmurs lettuce, with a leafy smile.

With flowers tipping hats so grand,
The sunflowers wave with golden hand.
They hold a riddle just for fun,
'Why did the beetroot refuse to run?'

So ponder deep in soil and shade,
The garden's jokes will never fade.
With laughter sprouting, plants unite,
In riddles woven, pure delight.

## Cultivating Curiosity

A curious bee buzzed with glee,
Exploring blooms on a summer spree.
"What's this plant? What's that one?"
The daisies echoed, "Let's have fun!"

A tomato plant, vibrant and red,
Took a swing with its leafy head.
"I've got the juiciest secret, though,
Come close and listen, don't be slow!"

The thyme sang songs, a fragrant tune,
While mint twirled under the bright moon.
"Each herb has tales of fancy and flight,
So stay awhile, let's party tonight!"

In laughter and whispers, the garden thrives,
With curious spirits, all life arrives.
So grab a spade and dig in deep,
From playful questions, magic leaps.

## Whispers of Wildflowers

In the garden, daisies dance,
With the bees in a silly trance.
Tulips giggle, bending low,
Saying hi to the worms below.

Crickets chirp their offbeat song,
While the daffodils hum along.
Frogs leap like they own the place,
Making faces in the muddy space.

Butterflies in a grand ballet,
Flap their wings in a vibrant play.
Every petal drops a smile,
As they bloom in a cheerful style.

And when the wind starts to tease,
All the flowers sway with ease.
Nature's laughter fills the air,
A comedic show for those who care.

## Infinite Corners of Nature

In the woods, squirrels plot and scheme,
Hiding acorns like a game of cream.
Mushrooms peek from under a hat,
As the raccoons practice their acrobat.

Birds argue over the best seat,
In the branches where the breezes meet.
A turtle in a slow race grins,
While the fox counts all its wins.

Rivers gurgle with a cheeky laugh,
As fish swim in their splashy bath.
The sun winks from a leafy nook,
While frogs write a very funny book.

Every corner whispers a joke,
From the smartest owl in a foggy cloak.
Nature's punchlines cover the ground,
In this comedy show, joys abound!

## **Luminescent Fruits of Labor**

Orchards shine with a fruity glow,
Apples gossip, putting on a show.
Pears gossip about the evening plan,
While the cherries compete in a can-can.

Bananas slip on their own peel,
Making oranges laugh with zeal.
Grapes cluster for a perfect pose,
While berries blush, nobody knows.

Fruits act out a silly spree,
In their harvest time jubilee.
Lemons try to crack a smile,
Citrus jokes that will last a while.

As twilight falls upon the land,
Fruits join hands, a merry band.
In the orchard, laughter rings,
Celebrating all the joy life brings.

## Seasons' Sacred Secrets

Spring whispers its tender tease,
Flaunting blooms like a gentle breeze.
Summer beams with a sunny grin,
While kids splash water, let the fun begin.

Autumn shuffles with a crunch,
Raking leaves, it's a playful lunch.
Winter giggles, hiding below,
In piles of snow, kids steal the show.

Every season bears a tale,
Of giggles, chuckles that never pale.
Nature's humor sways like a tree,
In every rustle, a melody free.

So dance with the seasons, join in the fun,
Where laughter weaves under the sun.
Nature's sacred joy, a grand affair,
Together we share, a bright world fair.

## The Blooming Odyssey

In a garden full of jest,
A cabbage wore a party vest.
The carrots danced with glee at night,
While radishes took flight in fright.

They planned a grand parade today,
But peas just wanted to play away.
With pickle balloons upon a string,
The whole farm laughed at everything.

Tomatoes joked with laughter bright,
Eggplants tried to take a bite.
Yet in the soil, beneath the fun,
Roots plotted their race to be the one.

Hands chuckled as they pulled weeds out,
While worms wiggled with joyful shout.
In this plot of cheerful mirth,
Life grows silly on this earth.

## Fertile Ground Beneath Our Feet

On fertile ground, the peas conspire,
To launch a joke, a wacky flyer.
With daisies dressed in silly hats,
They giggle at the dancing cats.

The corn is tall, it can't stop bragging,
While carrots giggle, a bit lagging.
"I'm the crunch!" the lettuce claimed,
As cucumbers posed, unashamed.

Each seedling shares a goofy tale,
Of sprouts that dream to set the sail.
With sunshine smiles and rain's sweet cheer,
Nature's slapstick spreads good cheer.

In the muck, where laughter thrives,
Life's a jest, where joy survives.
So let's embrace this silly spree,
For laughter roots us, can't you see?

## Springs of Possibility

In springs where veggies poke their heads,
Chards tell jokes and share their threads.
Zucchini's got a bouncing groove,
While radicchio finds its dance move.

The broccoli's a little shy,
But tells a pun that makes me cry.
Tomatoes rolling, red with laughter,
Giggling at the silly disaster.

With drip-drop rains to make them smile,
They're plotting fun, though it's worthwhile.
Cucumbers snap, "Let's start a game!"
While peppers yell, "Let's spread the fame!"

With roots all tangled, yet so spry,
Nature's humor is so spry.
A garden with a playful flair,
A place where joy is everywhere.

## Serenades of the Sowing

In nightly plots, the seeds take flight,
They sing along under the moonlight.
A tomato strums a tiny lute,
While carrots dance in their root suit.

Scarecrows join their merry throng,
Arms waving like they're singing a song.
"Let's grow a chorus," says the corn,
And soon, the whole field's brightly reborn!

With whispers of wind, they weave a tale,
Of sprouts that dream of ships to sail.
Beneath the stars, the laughter sows,
As daisies share their poetic prose.

In every burrow, under the dirt,
Life hums along with a happy flirt.
So join the jam, come take a chance,
In this garden of merry dance!

## A Tapestry of Bounty

In my garden, weeds hold hands,
Dancing wild in all their strands.
Tomatoes rolled like little balls,
While squirrels plan their veggie heists and thralls.

Carrots giggle beneath the dirt,
Trying hard to hide their spurt.
Eggplants wear their purple best,
While radishes invite the rest.

A scarecrow donning my old clothes,
Makes the crows laugh; you can suppose.
Zucchini hide, so round and shy,
While I've just tripped over pie.

Yet here I am, with muddy shoes,
Planting seeds of silly muse.
Harvest laughter, let's not frown,
We're all rooting for our clowning crown!

## Golden Threads in the Soil

My garden's like a circus show,
Where bugs parade and cacti glow.
Sunflowers wink with cheeky glee,
While ants file past like tiny bees.

The pumpkins wear their festive hats,
While carrots chat with sassy rats.
Beets blush red with quite the flair,
Puns and tales fill the air.

Kale grooves with a funky twist,
While I'm here, trying to resist.
Mud on my cheek, I strike a pose,
As bunnies scurry, wearing bow ties and bows!

We've planted jokes along the rows,
With every laugh, the garden grows.
In this patch, fun runs wild and free,
Digging deep for humor's jubilee!

**Fertile Imagination**

In the dirt, I find dreams sprout,
As pickles ponder what it's about.
Lettuce laughs with crunchy cheer,
While radish raves, "Let's have a beer!"

The peppers gossip, red and green,
Making salsa from a scene unseen.
Garlic winks, adds spice to the tale,
While pumpkins plot to sail and scale.

In rows, the herbs are quite divine,
Basil's pranks surely intertwine.
Time to plant this goofy plot,
With every seed, there's laughter caught.

So here I sow, with heart and soul,
Finding joy in every hole.
Let imagination freely bloom,
As veggies sway in vibrant room!

## Twilight Blossoms

Under twinkling stars, I roam,
With flower pots my silly home.
Daisies dance, while violets tease,
As moonlight spills with earthy breeze.

At dusk, my onions tell a joke,
While tulips blush, like they just woke.
Lemon trees crack citrus smiles,
Preparing fun for endless miles.

The strawberries sing a tune so sweet,
While beets boast bold in their seat.
In the twilight, joy takes flight,
As blossoms giggle through the night.

Here in my patch, the laughter flows,
With every bloom, the garden knows.
Let whimsy rule the evening air,
For in this soil, we all share!

## Journeying Through Lush Horizons

Past the bushes and tall weeds,
I tripped on roots, oh how it leads!
A squirrel laughed as I fell down,
Now I'm wearing nature's crown.

Bright fruits dangle, daring my reach,
Bananas wave, like they're at a beach.
With every step, a sneaky vine,
Wraps around my leg—it's just divine!

I thought I'd found a hidden stash,
But it's a gnome with a little mustache.
He winked at me, said, "Just relax!"
While flossing with a bunch of snacks.

A path of berries, red and blue,
By the way, I think I'm lost, don't you?
But every twist, a joke appears,
Laughing as I munch on pears.

## Chasing Sunbeams and Shadows

I ran after a beam of light,
But it giggled and took flight.
Caught in a dance with buzzing bees,
Stung by laughter, oh such a tease!

A shadow played hide and seek,
Behind the tree, that's quite a sneak!
I slipped and slid on soft, damp grass,
Look, the sun's now got my class!

As I chased, I tripped on air,
Landed in a patch—oh what despair!
But wildflowers winked, said, "Stay awhile!"
And offered comfort with their style.

Sunshine and giggles mix and blend,
On this wild journey, there's no end.
Just chase the rays and laugh away,
Because shadows can't make us sway!

## The Symphony of Ripening Time

Grapes are singing, oh such cheer,
Their juicy notes bring joy, my dear!
The lemons dance with sour delight,
Twirling in a zesty flight.

The apples plot to paint the trees,
In shades that would bring anyone to sneeze.
They jive to tunes of sweetened rhyme,
Every crunch, a step in time.

Bananas start their comedy show,
Peeling away, they steal the show.
While oranges giggle in their zest,
Citrus comedy, they're the best!

Let the harvest play its song,
As fruits and veggies dance along.
With every bite, a melody's found,
In this wacky garden—expressly sound!

## **Branching Out in Faith**

I climbed a tree that promised fruit,
But found a raccoon in a cute suit.
He bowed politely, offered me a snack,
Said, "Branch out, friend! There's no looking back!"

With every branch, a laugh appears,
As I share my dreams and silly fears.
Nuts and berries, all in delight,
Chasing the birds, oh what a sight!

A leap of faith, I tried so hard,
But ended up in the neighbor's yard.
Cats just stared, gave me the glance,
I winked back, and we joined the dance.

So here I am, in leafy peace,
Climbing high, my worries cease.
With every twist and turn I find,
Life's a funny tree—so unwind!

**Corners of Culmination**

In the corner shop, where dreams are sold,
A pickle danced, and a carrot got bold.
Bananas wore hats, all colors and gleam,
Life's juicy laughter was a comic theme.

A tomato tripped over its own red feet,
Wobbling like jelly, what a marvelous feat!
Lemons joined in, with a zesty cheer,
Who knew fruits had such comedic flair here?

An apple juggled oranges with flair and skill,
While grapes formed a band, what a quirky thrill!
Peppers cracked jokes that made onions cry,
In this fruity circus, laughter would fly!

So let's toast to the corners where silliness reigns,
In the garden of laughter, no room for pains.
A fruity assembly with humor supreme,
Life's little morsels are ripe for the dream!

## The Tapestry of Tended Dreams

Weaving together our hopes and our woes,
A vine with ambition, oh how it grows!
Lettuce sorted gossip from radishes round,
In the soil of life, hilarious truths are found.

Sunflowers debated the silliest trends,
While beans formed a crew, making new friends.
A shy little cabbage sought wisdom from bees,
"Why'd the onion cross roads?" "To plant more leaves!"

Lemons spoke softly with a high-pitched alarm,
"Mango, don't flirt, you're just too much charm!"
While herbs elegantly bowed, sipping on tea,
Their snickers echoed, sweet jubilee.

So here's to the fabric where chuckles entwine,
In the garden of folly, we'll endlessly dine.
Each stitch a delight, each plot grows a song,
In this sunny patch, we all laugh along!

## Footprints in an Emerald Glade

In the glade of green, where the veggies run wild,
A carrot wore sneakers, oh such a strange child!
Potatoes played hide-and-seek near an oak,
While a wise old pumpkin shared puns, what a joke!

Cucumbers marching in disco parade,
Dance moves so funky, nature's grand charade.
Chickpeas chuckled, rolling on the ground,
In this leafy wonder, mirth does abound.

A beet drew a map to the funniest route,
Laughing at all the silliness about.
"Watch out for puddles!" the romaine would say,
In this glade of giggles, let's frolic and play!

With each silly footprint that marks leafy trails,
The essence of joy grows, and laughter prevails.
So skip through the greens with a smile so bright,
In this emerald haven, all troubles take flight!

## Landscapes of Unbroken Growth

In fields of whimsy, where laughter takes root,
The cabbage started a band, oh what a hoot!
Carrots in sunglasses sang to the skies,
While broccoli danced, oh, what a surprise!

Beans told tall tales of their escapades,
"Nobody knows how to dodge tomato raids!"
Radishes chuckled at their own spicy deeds,
In this patch of humor, everyone succeeds.

The corn held a party beneath the great sun,
While fruits cracked wise about who's number one.
Melons rode waves on a giant leaf boat,
In this landscape of laughter, not one sad note!

So gather 'round friends, in this playful embrace,
Where growth isn't serious, just a happy space.
Join in the fun, let the good times roll,
In these wacky terrains, there's room for the soul!

## Palate of the Universe

An apple asked a pear for a bite,
But the pear was busy, feeling quite right.
The banana slipped in with a cheesy grin,
Saying, "Don't mind me, I'm just here for the win."

A grape rolled past on a juice-sloshed spree,
He tripped on his friends, all in jubilee.
"You squished my plans!" yelled an orange so bright,
As they laughed and danced through the cosmic night.

Lemons squeezed out some jokes to be told,
While cherries just giggled, feeling so bold.
In this tangy circus, they tossed up their cares,
Creating a jam as they spun through the airs.

The fruits in a frenzy, what a wild show,
Each color and flavor, a fabulous glow.
With laughter so ripe, they wove tales of glee,
In a universe steeped in sweet harmony.

## The Whispering Garden

In a garden where nectar sweet whispers flow,
A carrot told stories of how plants can grow.
The radish replied with a sprightly little jig,
"I've seen roots dance, while you sip on your swig!"

A basil leaf chuckled, as sunbeams did play,
"I spice up the air, what else can I say?"
As tomatoes rolled in, blushing so red,
They pranced like the stars, waking dreams from their bed.

Cucumbers whispered, with secrets to share,
"We grow in the shadows, enjoying the air."
A broccoli hieroglyph, green and absurd,
Claimed hidden meanings in each veggie word.

In this silly plot, all the veggies relate,
They plotted and planned to be funnier mates.
With humor they thrived, in the garden's embrace,
Finding joy in each sprout, in this lively place.

## Pilgrimage to Abundance

On a quest for the goods, a berry brigade,
They joined in a search for the freshest parade.
A traveler sighed, with a strawberry grin,
"Who knew finding fortune could be such a win!"

Off they all went, with baskets in tow,
Through fields of delight where the cheery winds blow.
A grape took the lead, with a map that was old,
Claiming hidden treasures and ripe fruits to hold.

An elder peach winked, with wisdom in skin,
"Life's sweetest journey is where fun begins!"
They stumbled on puddles that seemed to explode,
With jelly-like laughter, they skipped down the road.

Their journey brimmed over with giggles and cheer,
As laughter grew louder, they scattered the fear.
In a bounty of joy, they arrived at their fate,
To discover that happiness is truly first-rate.

## **Tangles of Verdant Hopes**

In a wild maze of greens, where seedlings complain,
Leaves had a meeting, discussing the rain.
"I'm wet and I'm wild!" squeaked a soggy sprout,
While peas rolled their eyes, blooming joys all about.

A sunflower beamed with a laugh in her face,
"You all need to chill! You're running this place!"
They tangled and twisted in botanical pranks,
With every green laughter, they filled up the banks.

A bush called for branches to join in a dance,
"Who cares about thorns? Let's take a chance!"
A hedgehog wiggled, with a soft-hearted grin,
"Embrace all your quirks! Let the fun times begin!"

Through the maze they marched, twirling wildly along,
Finding cheer in the chaos, they sang their own song.
In every corner, each leaf found its groove,
In a tangle of hopes, their spirits would move.

## Ambling through the Grove

In the grove where bananas dance,
The oranges smile at every chance.
A pear told a joke, the apples rolled,
While cherries giggled, stories retold.

A dancing kiwi, with shoes too tight,
Slipped on a grape, what a silly sight!
Lemons squeezed laughs as they waved around,
Peaches blushed bright when they hit the ground.

Underneath trees, the shadows play,
Mangoes decide to monopolize the day.
While watermelons hatched a grand scheme,
To turn the grove into a fruit-themed dream.

Berries bounced in their berry-patch dance,
Pineapples stayed calm, gave dreams a chance.
And just when you thought they'd take a break,
Here come the apples with a cake to bake!

## Colorful Constellations

Stars of fruit hang in the sky,
Bananas stretch out, oh so high.
Grapes twinkle like they've found a wish,
While strawberries giggle and swish and swish.

Peaches discuss who's the juiciest one,
Lemons crack jokes, always having fun.
One watermelon moon, round and bright,
Reflects in puddles, what a funny sight!

Raspberries argue who's best in the night,
While figs throw a party, oh what a fright!
A comet of citrus zooms through the scene,
Chasing blueberries, so fast and so keen.

With laughter and cheer in the cosmic play,
Fruit constellations brighten the way.
As night turns to dawn, they bid their goodbyes,
Waiting for nightfall to light up the skies.

## **Roots and Revelations**

Roots of knowledge underfoot,
Bananas pondering, "What's a fruit?"
Mangos pondering, "Where's my crown?"
While oranges laugh and roll around.

"Why is life sticky?" the pineapples muse,
"Are we just snacks, or do we choose?"
Nuts cracking jokes to lighten the load,
While radishes plan an underground road!

A wise old tree shared secrets of yore,
"Life's a buffet, not just a chore.
So take your time, and laugh a lot,
Fruitful moments are always sought!"

Rooted in laughter, twining in cheer,
Fruits united, they persevere.
Discovering joy from the ground to the skies,
With roots in giggles, they learn to rise.

## **Spheres of Influence**

Citrus circles plotting their schemes,
While apples debate the nature of dreams.
Bananas in suits making business calls,
Figuring out how to bounce off walls.

Pineapples with crowns think they're so grand,
While watermelons roll through the land.
Grapes hold a conference, grape juice in tow,
Conspiring ways to steal the show.

In the sphere of fruit, the discussion is rife,
Who can make the most out of this life?
With laughter exploding like seeds in the sun,
These fruity pals are always having fun!

So raise your glass to the juicy brigade,
In the orchard, their plans are made.
For in every fruit, there's a joke and a laugh,
Creating the sphere of a perfect path!

## **Wayfarer's Abundance**

A traveler strolls with laughter loud,
Chasing pigeons and lost in a crowd.
He spots a fruit stand, oh what a sight,
Bananas in pajamas, quite the delight!

With apples that giggle in merry display,
He juggles them all in a comical way.
Peaches that chuckle, they fall from the tree,
"Pick me, pick me, there's plenty of me!"

His wallet is light, but his heart is full,
As grapes roll away like a jolly ol' fool.
He dances with berries, each step like a song,
While cherries cheer on, "Come join us, along!"

With every fresh bite, he grins ear to ear,
In a world full of flavors, there's nothing to fear.
For joy is the harvest, ripe on the vine,
And laughter the fruit that's simply divine!

## Curry of Colors

In the kitchen, a pot boils with cheer,
Colors collide like a carnival here.
Turmeric twirls in a playful dance,
While cumin sneezes—oh, what a chance!

Red pepper flakes sprinkle like stars,
"Try to keep up!" the garlic one spars.
Onions do waltzes, the carrots parade,
It's a vibrant affaire, no color will fade!

Lentils in masquerade, so round and so round,
Popping with laughter, they're joyfully found.
With every big scoop that he takes with a grin,
He swirls the spoon 'round—it's fun to dig in!

At dinner time, everyone jumps in delight,
Sharing the curry, making it bright.
No waste here tonight, just laughter and bliss,
In this pan of colors, no flavor to miss!

**Petals on the Trail**

Wandering flowers stroll down the way,
"Stop and smell us!" they giggle and sway.
Daisies and tulips in a game of tag,
With bees throwing pollen—it's quite the brag!

"Did you see that bloom, it nearly took flight!"
A rose blushed red, said, "I'm feeling so bright!"
Sunflowers tower, giving a wink,
"Join us for fun, let's dance on the brink!"

Petals greet hikers with whispers of cheer,
"Follow our path, you'll find treasures here."
With each little step, a giggle released,
Nature's own garden, a laughing feast!

So come join the fun on this colorful ride,
With flowers as friends, there's joy to abide.
To skip and to laugh, is the secret we find,
In the petals we leave, leave all worries behind!

**Paths Woven in Harvest**

Through fields of green where laughter rolls,
Farmers harvest giggles, that's how it goes.
"Grab a basket, let's make a scene!"
With corn on the cob acting all keen!

Pumpkins are plotting a Halloween spree,
"We're not just for pies, come dance with me!"
The squash shakes its roots, "What's taking so long?"
It's a merry old harvest, let's sing a new song!

The carrots are waiting in rows on parade,
"Pick me, pick me!" they chant unafraid.
As cucumbers giggle, they roll off the shelf,
"Join in the fun, don't be like a kelp!"

With baskets in hand and smiles a-bright,
This harvest day is pure delight.
From laughter-filled fields to kitchens of cheer,
These paths we have woven are joyous my dear!

**Pollen in the Wind**

Bees buzz around with a silly dance,
They wiggle and jiggle, not missing a chance.
A flower's a party, come one, come all,
With pollen to throw, we'll have a grand ball.

The dandelions laugh as they float through the air,
Spreading their fluff without a single care.
"Catch me if you can!" they taunt with a grin,
As we chase down the breeze, let the fun begin!

Each blossom's a friend, each petal a joke,
The garden's our stage; it's a comedy cloak.
With nectar so sweet, you'll laugh even more,
Join in the fun, what's behind flower's door?

So if you're feeling low, take joy from the hive,
Dance with the bees, feel the laughter revive.
For nature's got humor, it flows like a stream,
Join in the antics and savor the dream!

## Whispers of the Harvest Moon

Under a moon that giggles and glows,
Vegetables chuckle, and the corn just knows.
The pumpkins are plotting a Halloween prank,
While silvery squash put on their best prank.

"Hey, did you hear the potatoes say?"
"They think they're on top, but they're buried away!"
The carrots are snickering, tucked in their beds,
While onions just cry, 'cause they're chopping their heads!

The harvest moon winks as it watches the scene,
Dancing with shadows, it's a funny routine.
Fruit flies in tuxedos all waddle in style,
Their tiny bowties make you laugh for a while.

So gather your friends, bring your laughter and cheer,
Join in the fun that's abundant each year.
When night falls in autumn, the giggles will bloom,
In the glow of the harvest, we banish all gloom!

## Harvesting Dreams

With each little dream, we plant in the night,
A garden of giggles begins to take flight.
We water our wishes with laughter and cheer,
And watch as they blossom throughout the whole year.

Sometimes they grow silly, with topsy-turvy vines,
Laughter spills out as they form strange designs.
A vegetable orchestra plays tunes in the sun,
While fruit on their branches play catch as a fun!

Collecting our hopes in a wacky old sack,
We take them downtown, and they're never too slack.
The carrots lead parades, the apples all cheer,
While tomatoes just blush, hiding year by year.

So when you feel down, just garden your heart,
Let joy grow like weeds, let's all play our part.
Harvesting dreams brings the silliness near,
Let laughter be your crop; it's time to adhere!

## Blossoms Beneath the Borealis

In the land of the north where the colors collide,
Blooms vanish and giggle, they take a wild ride.
Under the auroras, they dance in delight,
Each petal a whisper that sparks in the night.

"Hey there, Mr. Tulip, come join our parade!"
But tulips just twirl, in a posy charade.
The daisies are plotting a sneaky balloon,
While stirring the nectar as sweet as a tune.

The frost may bring laughs, in a cold winter's hug,
But blossoms keep dreaming, like a cheerful bug.
They think they'll play tricks as the snowflakes swirl,
With giggles and chuckles, they whirl and they twirl.

So if you feel chilly, just look to the sky,
Join flowers and laughter, let your dreams fly high.
Beneath the borealis, they jest and they play,
In the heart of each blossom, let fun lead the way!

## Echoing in the Wilderness

In the woods, a squirrel dances,
Chasing its tail, taking his chances.
Whispering trees giggle with glee,
As rabbits play hide and seek, oh me!

A bear in a hat tries to sing,
While ducks in a line do their thing.
Frogs jump and croak, a lively show,
Who knew the woods had such a flow?

A porcupine shows off his spines,
Twisting and turning, oh how he shines!
Meanwhile, a moose joins the parade,
With socks on his hooves, oh what a charade!

As night falls, the owls take flight,
They hoot out jokes that feel just right.
Echoes of laughter fill the air,
In this wild place, without a care.

## Ferns Beneath the Starlight

Under twinkling stars, ferns sway,
A raccoon steals snacks, makes his play.
The moon winks down, a playful glance,
As creatures join in a midnight dance.

Crickets chirp with rhythmic glee,
While fireflies flicker, oh so free.
Hopping frogs lead the crazy conga,
As owls scratch heads, asking 'What's a bonga?'

A hedgehog in shades grins wide,
Says, "Join my crew and take a ride!"
Sprinting past trees and soft lilacs,
They giggle and tumble without tracks.

With laughter echoing through the night,
These forest friends are pure delight.
Underneath the stars they revel,
In a world where fun takes the level.

## Winding through Fields of Wonder

A rabbit rides on a bicycle,
Wobbling left and right, oh, what a spectacle!
Twirling daisies cheer him on,
While butterflies flutter, a colorful dawn.

In fields of clover, a dance-off emerges,
Between a goat and a cow, who surges?
Grasshoppers judge, with tiny wigs,
While ducks quack in rhythm, doing jigs!

A pig in a tutu prances about,
With a twirl and a spin, no shadow of doubt.
"Life's a party!" he squeals with a trot,
While chickens join in, giving all they've got.

As the sun sets, laughter fills the air,
In every corner, joy everywhere.
For in these fields, with silliness abound,
True happiness is always found.

**Tasting the Horizons**

An apple pie fell from the sky,
With a twist and a spin, oh my, oh my!
A donut cloud floats, what a sight,
As sprinkles rain down with pure delight!

A fruit bat says, "Hey, let's BBQ!"
With pineapple slices, it's a jammin' stew.
Bananas laugh as they're peeled with grace,
While cherries compete in a rolling race.

The stars wink down on this fruity scene,
As oranges juggle, what a routine!
Berries burst forth with giggly squeals,
Making smoothies that spin like wheels.

With each sip, the world lifts higher,
Taste buds tingle, fueling the fire.
In this land where flavor reigns low,
The horizons beckon with joy in tow.

## Eco-Expedition

In the jungle, I trip on a vine,
Banana peels make me feel fine.
A parrot squawks, 'You're lost, my friend!'
I laugh and say, 'Is this the end?'

The bugs in my backpack start to sing,
They dance like it's a wild fling.
With each step, I ponder my fate,
Maybe I'll find a way to relate!

A monkey throws fruit right in my face,
He thinks it's all just a big race.
I dodge and weave, it's quite a sight,
Nature's antics keep me light!

So here I roam, in nature's embrace,
Learning to laugh, in this crazy place.
Adventure awaits in every crack,
With each giggle, I'll never look back!

## Silence of the Trees

In a forest deep, I hear a sneeze,
Is that a ghost, or just the trees?
They giggle softly, their leaves a-flutter,
Whispering jokes, all in a mutter.

A wise old oak starts to yawn,
'You humans walk like a herd of fawn!'
I chuckle, thinking, 'What do they know?'
But I trip over roots, oh what a show!

Sap drips down, like nature's glue,
Or is it just the trees' way to spew?
'You're sticky now,' the pine tree laughs,
'Enjoy these moments, they multiply in halves!'

But even trees know how to play,
With branches swaying, they stole my way.
I dance around, as if I'm free,
In the silence of trees, I found comedy!

## Mosaics of Nature's Larder

A picnic spread on a grassy patch,
Ants march in, nature's little batch.
'Excuse me, sirs!' I keenly shout,
'Not invited—please, wait it out!'

Mushrooms dance like they're on a spree,
A gathering of friends, all wild and free.
I dip in a dip; it's wild and cheesy,
Nature's buffet isn't always easy!

Berries burst like tiny balloons,
Squirrels are dancing, humming tunes.
I slip on a berry, slide like a seal,
Nature's kitchen has a funny appeal!

So let the wild flavors do their thing,
Life's a dish worth a hearty sing.
Each bite a giggle, each crunch a cheer,
Mosaics of laughter that we revere!

## **Glimmers of Unseen Potential**

In a garden spot where weeds like to roam,
Sprouts whisper secrets, feeling at home.
'What's your plan?' asks the sunflower tall,
'To grow a mansion, or just play ball?'

Potatoes hide, like they're in a game,
Shouting, 'We're rocks! Please, don't find our name!'
Carrots wiggle, pretending to dance,
'This garden party's got a strange romance!'

Bees buzz by, with gossip to share,
'Have you heard? The tomatoes have flair!'
Squash joins in, 'We're fabulous and bright,'
While I just laugh, trying to take flight.

So in this patch, potential is grand,
With humor blooming from every strand.
Lessons learned in the gardening quest,
Laughter and green, truly the best!

**Trails of Abundance**

In the garden where laughter thrives,
Chickens wearing hats do high-fives.
Beans grow taller than a man,
While carrots play a funky band.

Gourds are rolling down the path,
Making everyone laugh with their math.
Radishes compete in a dance-off,
While squashes giggle and then scoff.

Tomatoes blush in the summer sun,
Telling jokes—oh, this is fun!
Peppers leap into a friendly race,
Chasing cucumbers with a grin on their face.

In this world of quirky cheer,
Gardens bloom, and smiles appear.
Each step brings a chuckle and cheer,
Serving up joy as the harvest draws near.

## Lanterns of Growth

In the night, the veggies shine bright,
A pumpkin winks with all its might.
Zucchinis dancing under the moon,
Carrots play a merry tune.

Garlic sways, it's quite the sight,
While onions giggle with pure delight.
Shining lanterns in garden beds,
Make the rabbits scratch their heads.

Basil tells tales from days of yore,
About herbs that tried to start a chore.
With laughter and joy filling the air,
The fruits and veggies have not a care.

Cabbages join in with a shout,
In this garden, there's no doubt.
Each sprout beams with holiday cheer,
Growing together, year after year.

## **Orchard of Dreams**

In an orchard where giggles bloom,
Apples dance, dispelling gloom.
Peaches wear sunglasses, looking cool,
While pears declare, 'Back to school!'

Cherries chatter in a sunny row,
Planning pranks on the people below.
Plums sing songs that twirl and swirl,
As bees join in with a busy whirl.

Lemons tell jokes that are quite sour,
While grapefruits flaunt their zesty power.
Each tree shakes with laughter and glee,
In this dreamland, everyone's free.

So come join the fruit's merry spree,
Where every harvest is filled with glee.
In an orchard where dreams take flight,
Laughter echoes until the night.

## Turning Leaves toward Light

Leaves are twirling, upside down,
Wearing bright hues, flipping around.
Beetles march in a funny parade,
While squirrels plan their next escapade.

Each leaf whispers a playful jest,
As sunbeams tickle it, what a quest!
Dancing shadows play on the ground,
Making funny faces all around.

Branches sway, telling silly tales,
Of runaway acorns in their trails.
As the breeze joins in for a laugh,
It's a garden of joy, every path.

So let's embrace this wondrous sight,
Turning leaves that reach for the light.
In this whimsical, jolly spree,
Nature's giggles are wild and free.

## **Roots Beneath**

Digging deep, I found some snacks,
Old potatoes and a bunch of flax.
Worms were dancing, oh what a sight,
Living life with glee, what a delight!

The carrots giggled, hiding in mud,
As I tripped over a gardening bud.
Plants all whispered their secret jokes,
While the radishes teased the stubborn oaks.

Roots entwined like a wild dance,
Trying to sway in the summer's prance.
They warned me of rain and told me to chill,
While I marveled at their underground thrill.

So here I sit, in this earthy scruff,
Tapping my roots, saying, "Life's pretty tough!"
But under this ground, where laughter flows,
A garden full of surprises grows.

## Sky Above

Clouds are giggling, look at that shape,
A sacred fruit with a banana cape!
The sun's a chef, grilling rays on high,
While birds drop jokes as they zoom by.

Blueberries bounce in the breeze so sweet,
Dancing to rhythms of nature's beat.
Each sunbeam tickles the apple trees,
Making them snicker in the summer breeze.

Light's shining down, like butter on bread,
Even the grapes are happy instead!
The wind's a messenger, whistling bright,
Carrying secrets of day and night.

So I lie back, with arms spread wide,
Laughing at clouds, feeling their pride.
In this sky of whimsy, I find my muse,
Every glance at nature fills me with views.

## The Alchemy of Blossoms

Blossoms burst forth like surprise confetti,
Trying to dance, but they're all getting petty.
A tulip whispers, 'Hey, did you hear? '
Last night's moon pulled a prank on a deer!

Petals are giggling, shades of delight,
Painting the world in colors so bright.
Who knew a lilac could snicker and sigh,
As bees buzzed by with a curious eye?

Sunflowers wise, with heads held so high,
Debate on nectar while passing by.
Laughter erupts from the daisies' embrace,
As they challenge the violets in this flowery race.

In this realm of blossoms, where humor grows,
Each flower knows how hilarity flows.
Join in the fun, let your spirits soar,
In the garden of laughter, there's always more!

## Currents of Orchard Winds

Orchard winds tickle the fruit on the vine,
Whispering secrets in each twist and twine.
Apples are chuckling, they're wise and round,
Sharing tales of the best pranks around.

The pears discuss plans to stage a play,
While grapes form a mob for a wild parade.
Each gentle breeze brings a message to share,
From the peaches who dream that they could fly in the air.

A breeze rolls through, full of laughter and cheer,
Even the oranges are rolling with fear!
"Why do we dangle, why don't we stand?
We're fruit with good taste, isn't life just grand?"

So let's sway with the branches, join in the fun,
As the orchard spins tales under the sun.
In the currents of laughter, we take our stand,
Hand in hand with fruit, a merry band!

## Gardens of Wanderlust

In gardens of dreams where oddities bloom,
A cucumber juggles, making room!
Tomatoes wear hats, all different shapes,
While carrots consult on their scruffy escapes.

I wander through rows of whimsical plots,
Giggling cucumbers and giggling plots.
Every leaf rustles with tales of their peaks,
Inviting all wanderers to share their freaks.

Herbs tell tall tales of spice and delight,
While radishes scheme for a dinner delight.
Zucchini dreams of a big old parade,
While peas patter, as more hope is laid.

This garden's alive, a festival bright,
Where laughter and joy spring forth day and night.
Join the festivities, no need for a map,
In this garden of wanderlust, giggles overlap!

## Harvesting Tomorrow

With a basket in hand and a grin,
I search for the treasures where weeds have been.
The apples are winking, the pears play coy,
I'll juggle them all, oh what a joy!

But then comes a squirrel, with a wink and a tail,
Stealing my bounty, oh what a fail!
He dances around like he's earned a degree,
I'll negotiate terms—hey, just share with me!

Carrots are hiding like they're playing cool,
Hiding from me as if I'm a fool.
I'll dig with a shovel, and perhaps a song,
Only to find they've been plotting all along!

So here's to the fun in tomorrow's quest,
With mischief and laughter, life feels the best.
I'll gather my harvest, though squirrels might pout,
With giggles and grins, we'll figure it out!

**Bounty of the Journey**

I wandered through fields of corn and beans,
Chasing the harvest, living my dreams.
Pickles in jars and bread on the rise,
Jars of jelly staring with jelly bean eyes!

On the path, I tripped on a vine,
Fell into beans, it must be a sign!
Could this be fate or merely good luck?
Turns out it's just my old friend, a truck!

With each step I take, I gather the loot,
A basket of treasures, some not quite astute.
But fruit cakes are laughing as I take a bite,
It crumbles and falls—it's a splendid sight!

So here in the garden where silliness blooms,
I'll dance with the zucchinis, in their green costumes.
Let's celebrate chaos with gusto and cheer,
For bounty awaits, now bring on the beer!

## Seeds of Serenity

Throwing some seeds in the light summer breeze,
Watching them scatter with grace and with ease.
They land in the wrong spots, what a silly show,
Those carrots are dancing, not wanting to grow!

Tomatoes are gossiping, they claim it's not fair,
That cucumbers get all the attention and flair.
"Let's form a union!" a lettuce shouts loud,
But the peas just giggle, they're terribly proud!

Fertilizer jokes, oh they sure make me laugh,
What did the corn say? It's a-maize-ing math!
They chat as they grow, each inch is a thrill,
Let's see who shimmies and jives on the hill!

So seeds, take your time, there's nothing to rush,
In the garden of giggles, we'll bask in the hush.
With laughter and joy, we'll grow side by side,
Planting our dreams, and enjoying the ride!

## **Blossoms of Resilience**

In the garden of hopes, blooms the flower of giggles,
Twirling in circles, it twitches and wiggles.
The sun plays peek-a-boo, clouds start to frown,
But petals just dance, they won't let us down!

A cactus complains that it feels quite alone,
While daisies insist that it should be shown.
"Throw some water!" they cheer and they laugh,
And he smiles 'cause that's when he gets to take a selfie graph!

The sunflowers stretch to brush the blue sky,
Waving their yellow, saying, 'Oh, me? Hi!'
With ants in a line, marching up to the peak,
They carry their burdens, though they're not supposed to squeak!

So here's to resilience, together we thrive,
With blooms of silliness, we're too fun to jive!
Laughter is plenty, and nature agrees,
We're all in this garden, growing with ease!

**Feasting on Experiences**

I went to feast on wisdom's dish,
But tripped and fell, oh what a wish!
The pies of laughter beckoned me,
While fruits of folly rolled with glee.

With every slice, I found surprise,
My thoughts just danced before my eyes.
A banquet rich in silly dreams,
I swallowed both, or so it seems!

The bread was warm, the soup was hot,
I laughed so hard, I forgot the pot!
Each nibble sparked unplanned delight,
A dinner party in full flight.

So here's to feasting, come what may,
With every gulp, I'll lose my way.
A buffet spruced with zest and cheer,
I'll dine on moments, far and near.

**Branches of Enlightenment**

Beneath the trees of bright, odd thought,
I climbed so high, forgot what's sought.
A branch of truth waved just for me,
But slipped my grip, oh what a spree!

The squirrels laughed, their nuts in tow,
While I was stuck in branches low.
I swayed with joy, a swinging fool,
In search of knowledge, made a stool.

The fruits above, so ripe and round,
Promised wisdom I had found.
But as I reached, they rolled away,
A game of chase turned bright as day.

So here I dangle, full of glee,
Grabbing thoughts from nutty trees.
Who needs the ground when you can sway?
With silly smiles, I'll find my way.

## Tides of Growth

The ocean waves, they pull and push,
Like dreams that swirl in fragrant hush.
I rode the surf of whacky chance,
With seaweed wrapped, I did a dance.

The tide rolled in with laughter's wave,
I dared to dive, to splash, to rave.
Each ripple sparkled with delight,
As fish joined in the silly fight.

The seashells sang a funny tune,
I twirled around beneath the moon.
Though tides may pull, I'll always float,
On waves of joy, a buoyant boat.

So here's to currents, wild and free,
Where growth brings giggles just for me.
With salty hair and sunburned glow,
I'll ride each wave, let laughter flow.

## Embracing the Abundant

In a garden where the veggies sing,
I snacked on veggies, what a fling!
Tomatoes danced, the carrots spry,
Each veggie teased a grinning eye.

The fruit trees giggled as they swayed,
With every bite, my whims displayed.
Peppers in jester hats so bright,
Made meals a carnival of light.

When greens unite, they make me play,
With broccoli tops that dare to sway.
I tossed my salad with a cheer,
It spun around, my heart sincere.

So here I munch, with joy so vast,
Embracing snacks, both big and fast.
In every crunch, a world I see,
With funny flavors calling me!

www.ingramcontent.com/pod-product-compliance
Lightning Source LLC
Chambersburg PA
CBHW070007300426
43661CB00141B/293